THE
CALIFORNIA
COAST

Featuring the Photography of Chris Swan

CLB 1253
Copyright © 1985 Illustrations and text: Colour Library Books Ltd.,
    Guildford, Surrey, England.
Display and text filmsetting by Acesetters Ltd.,
    Richmond, Surrey, England.
Produced by AGSA, in Barcelona, Spain.
Color separations by Llovet, S.A., Barcelona, Spain.
Printed and bound in Barcelona, Spain by Rieusset and Eurobinder.
All rights reserved.
Published 1985 by Crescent Books, distributed by Crown Publishers, Inc.
Printed in Spain.
ISBN 0 517 462887
h g f e d c b a

THE
CALIFORNIA COAST

Text by
MARVIN KARP

CRESCENT BOOKS
NEW YORK

It is a land of contradictions, extremes and uniqueness. It is a land that nature endowed with unrivaled beauty along a stretch of Pacific coastline called Big Sur, and then counterbalanced it with a bleak, inhospitable environment called Death Valley.

It is a land where the oldest and tallest living things on earth, the towering, 3,000-year-old redwood trees and sequoias stand in solemn splendor, defying the ravages of time and weather. It is also a land where the odors from primeval tar pits, which are still yielding evidence of life 40,000 years ago, mingle with man-made air pollution in downtown Los Angeles.

It is a place where fads, fashion and fantasy are important staples of the economy. And for some inexplicable reason, it has become the cradle of esoteric religious sects, and cults advocating alternative life styles.

To a large segment of its population, it is a state of mind. To the rest of the world, it is the State of California.

Nicknamed the Golden State, California leads its sister states in many categories, and if it were a separate country, it would rank among the top nations in the Western world. It is interesting to note that the first European discoverers of California believed this Pacific Coast land mass to be an island. If fact, the name "California" was taken from a 16th century romance novel by the Spanish writer Ordonez de Montalvo. In it, a mythical female warrior queen named Califia ruled an island of gold called California. Such was the beginning of the California mystique.

According to modern-day ecologists, there is more to the idea of California being an island than just the miscalculation of some Spanish conquistadores or a writer's fairy tale. Nature isolated California geographically and geologically by bounding it with mountains and desert on one side and the ocean on the other. This has resulted in the development of distinctive, and in some cases unique, spcies of plant and animal life. For example, the giant condor and the redwood tree exist only in California... and there are many other unique species of flora and fauna.

The geologic history of the earth, dating from pre-Cambrian times millions of years ago right up to the present Cenozoic Era, can be read in the cliffs and canyons of the state. And scientists have identified more than 500 separate soil species, which include most of the soil groups found throughout the world.

Roughly rectangular in shape, with a generally north-to-south configuration for much of its length, California extends through nearly ten degrees of latitude, which means that if it were located on the East Coast, it would stretch from Cape Cod in Massachusetts down to Charleston, South Carolina. It measures about 780 miles in length through the center of the state, with 1,264 miles of coastline. Its width runs from 150 to 350 miles and its total land area is approximately 158,700 square miles, putting it in third place among the 50 states in total area, behind Alaska and Texas. San Bernardino County, however, claims the title as the largest county in the United States. It covers more than 20,000 square miles, an area almost as large as Connecticut, Massachusetts and New Jersey put together.

Trivia buffs will be interested in knowing that about three-quarters of the way down the California coastline, just north of Los Angeles, the land bends eastward. Because of this shift in direction, the City of Angels is actually located east of Reno, Nevada, and the city of San Diego is on a line with the western border of Idaho.

Among its geologic inheritances, California can claim the *highest* elevation in the conterminous United States, Mount Whitney, which soars 14,494 feet above sea level, and the *lowest* point in the hemisphere, a forsaken spot named Bad Water, in Death Valley, 282 feet below sea level. Incidentally, both of these areas can be viewed from the same location; a 5,400-foot mountain called Dante's View about three miles east of Death Valley.

Death Valley has two other distinctions worth mentioning. The highest temperature ever recorded in the United States, 134°F., was reported there on July 10, 1913. Readings of 130°F. are not uncommon. What is uncommon, however, is the residence built by a rugged old prospector named Walter E. Scott. Death Valley Scotty lived there for 30 years and left behind a cluster of Spanish-style buildings known as Scotty's Castle, a monument to his ability to adapt to the environment and make his home where few others could.

Because of its north-south range, California offers a great diversity of climate and temperature. The northern and central coasts enjoy relatively mild climates, though the temperatures are generally lower than those along the southern coast. But moving eastward to the Sierra Nevada, the temperature drops sharply, often reaching zero and below. It was at the town of Boca, on the eastern slope of the Sierra Nevada, that a reading of -45°F. was recorded on January 20, 1937, the lowest in the history of the state. This is the area where a yearly snowfall of 450 inches is not unusual. The northern coast does not get snow very often, and snowfall is even rarer along the central and southern coasts.

Temperatures in the southern part of the state, from Santa Barbara to Mexico, run from mild along the coast to extremely hot moving eastward toward the desert areas.

Just as there are extremes in temperature, so too are there extremes in precipitation. Rainfall along the northern coast averages nore than 80 inches a year, with the all-time high of 190 inches at Honeydew. It falls off to an inch or two at most in the southeastern desert regions. One spot in Death Valley went without measurable precipitation for 760 days, a record that no other place in the United States has ever matched.

For the most part, California has only two distinct seasons, a rainy season and a dry season. The curious thing about the rainy season is that it does not occur during the summer, which is the time most areas of the world receive their greatest rainfall. Summer in California, especially in the southern portion, is dry, a time when the land becomes parched, making it vulnerable to devastating brush and forest fires.

The rainy season in California runs from October to April in the north, and from November to March or April further south, with the rainiest month being January.

Climate plays a vital role in the lives of the state's three largest cities, San Francisco, Los Angeles and San Diego. As the northernmost of the three, San Francisco is built on the hills fronting a great natural bay, and the breezes off the water give it temperatures that range from about 50°F. in January to an average of 59°F. in July. During the summer months of July and August, San Francisco is probably the coolest large city in the United States. San Franciscans delight in their climate, claiming it gives them more energy and makes the city more vital.

Los Angeles also lies near the sea, and being several hundred miles south of San Francisco, its climate is warmer and drier. An unfortunate combination of climate, location and air pollution from too many cars has made Los Angeles the victim of smog that smothers the city with a yellow tinge and an acrid smell from time to time. It gets relief when a good rain cleanses the air, or a strong breeze from the sea blows the smog away.

San Diego, about 16 miles from the Mexican border town of Tijuana, is the driest of the three coastal cities, with only about 10 inches of rainfall annually. It has the balmiest climate, the clearest air and the most sunshine. San Diego is the fortunate recipient of a unique natural gift – a ridge of high-pressure air over the North Pacific called the Hawaiian High holds back weather from San Diego that affects other parts of the California coast. At the same time, morning clouds and sea breezes keep the temperatures moderate and help make the area a mecca for vacationers and retirees.

The first visitors to California are believed to have been migratory tribes who crossed the Bering land bridge from Asia to Alaska and then turned south. That happened about 35-40,000 years ago, and the La Brea Tar Pits in Los Angeles are still giving up evidence of their existence. It was not until the mid-16th century, however, that Europeans discovered the area and altered for all time the tranquil isolation that the inhabitants enjoyed.

In 1542, a Portuguese navigator, Juan Rodriguez Cabrillo, was employed by the Spanish viceroy of Mexico to search the coast north of Baja California for the Strait of Anian, a supposed shortcut between Europe and China around the top of North America. Cabrillo died during his quest, and his pilot, Bartolomeo Ferrelo, continued the exploration as far north as the present border between California and Oregon. Ferrelo found neither the long-sought strait nor anything else of value. What he did encounter were rough seas, a mountainous coastline and hostile Indians.

A little more than a quarter of a century later, Francis Drake, after raiding several Pacific coast towns in South America and capturing a Spanish treasure ship loaded with silver ingots, headed north. He dropped anchor at Drake's Bay, which is now part of Point Reyes National Seashore, just a few miles north of San Francisco. He spent time repairing his ship, the *Golden Hinde*, claimed the area for his country and Queen Elizabeth I and, after naming it Nova Albion, he set sail for England. In 1937, a brass plate which he purportedly left behind as evidence of his claim was found in the area where Drake had made camp. The authenticity of the marker is still under investigation.

Strange as it may seem today, neither the Spanish nor the English made any real effort to colonize California. It was almost 200 years after Drake's visit that the Spaniards, fearful that Russia might have designs on California, sent an expedition northward by land to establish missions and presidios (forts) and to discourage the Russians from encroaching.

In 1769, Gaspar de Portola, the governor of Baja California, led the land expedition, accompanied by Father Junipero Serra, a Franciscan monk. They established the first settlement, Mission San Diego de Alcala, near the site of present-day San Diego. Portola continued up the coast to Monterey Bay, where he established a fort, and a few years later settlers built the village of Yerba Buena (now known as San Francisco) on the bay.

Between 1770 and 1823, Father Serra and his successors built a chain of 21 Franciscan missions stretching from San Diego to Sonoma, each one just a day's walk from the next. The path connecting these missions became known as El Camino Real, California's first highway. Today, the state has the most complex system of freeways in the world. And it ranks only behind the entire countries of the United States, France and the United Kingdom in the number of motor vehicles using those roads.

Despite Spain's attempt at a show of force, the Russians sent a contingent down from Sitka, Alaska, in 1812, and built Fort Ross, a fortified village, about 80 miles north of San Francisco Bay near Bodega Bay. Their intention was to grow food for their Alaskan settlements, to trade with the Spanish Californians and expand their sea otter and seal hunting operations into Spanish waters. The Russian efforts were not successful, however, and under continual pressure from both Mexico and the United States, which had proclaimed the Monroe Doctrine in 1821, they agreed to limit their expansion to Alaska. Twenty years later (1841), they sold Fort Ross and everything in it to a Swiss settler named Johann A. Sutter, the man at whose mill gold would be discovered seven years later. The only reminders that the Russians had ever settled in California are the partially restored fort, and the Russian River, which flows to the sea a few miles from it.

Following the trail blazed by the Franciscans and the soldiers came settlers from Mexico and Spain. And before the end of the 18th century, the first American ship from the East, the *Otter*, appeared off the California coast. Soon, American merchantmen were a common sight in California ports.

Meanwhile, the Spanish Colonials in Mexico were beginning to resent the heavy hand of their Spanish sovereign. Taking a lesson from their neighbors to the north, they rebelled against Spain in 1821 and won their freedom. California then became a province of Mexico

Several years later, a party of trappers led by Jedediah Smith became the first Americans to reach California via an overland route through the deserts from Utah, to San Gabriel Mission near Los Angeles. This opened the way for other trappers and explorers, and by 1841, the first organized group of American settlers reached California by land. They were followed by long wagon trains of pioneers wanting to settle in the sun.

The influx of Americans kept growing, and as their numbers increased so did their reluctance to accept the laws and government of Mexico, thereby creating a widening rift between the two peoples. This situation was further aggravated by the appearance of Captain John Charles Fremont of the U.S. Corps of Topographical Engineers, who led two parties of surveyors into California between 1844 and 1846.

At one point, the Mexicans ordered Fremont to break up his camp near Monterey and leave the territory. In defiance, Fremont moved about 25 miles away, raised the American flag over Hawk's Peak and began to build a small fort. Open conflict was averted when Fremont pulled out under cover of darkness. The date was March, 1846. Two months later, troops of the United States and Mexico clashed along the Rio Grande River in Texas, the disputed boundary between the two countries. War had begun.

News of the outbreak of war had not reached northern California by June of 1846 when a band of American trappers and settlers decided to take matters into their own hands. They captured Mexico's headquarters at Sonoma and raised their own homemade flag over the fort. The flag had a single star, a grizzly bear and the inscription "California Republic," which led the action to be known thereafter as the Bear Flag Revolt.

The Mexican-American War was relatively short-lived, and the conquest of California by U.S. soldiers, sailors and marines fairly easy. Under the Treaty of Guadalupe Hidalgo, signed on February 2, 1848, Mexico gave up California along with New Mexico and Arizona.

By a curious twist of fate, just a little less than two weeks before the peace treaty was signed, gold was discovered in the American River at the sawmill owned by Johann Augustus Sutter. That started a migration to California that has continued right up to today, making it the most populous state in the nation, according to the 1980 census. With a head count of about 24,000,000, California has more people than over 100 countries in the world.

Sutter had come to America from Switzerland in the 1830s and headed for California. In 1839, he received a large land grant in the Sacramento Valley from Mexico and built a fort and trading post which he named "New Helvetia." It was the first outpost of white civilization in inland California. Sutter hired James Marshall, a carpenter, to find an appropriate site for a sawmill and build one there. Marshall picked a site at Coloma on the American River, about 45 miles from the fort, and began construction. It was while inspecting the millrace on or about January 24, 1848, that he noticed a shiny, pea-sized stone in the ditch. Retrieving it from the water along with some others like it, Marshall went back to the fort, where he and Sutter tested the pebbles. All tests indicated that they were gold.

Despite the efforts of both men to keep the news quiet, word of the gold discovery began to spread, with the final confirmation coming from President James Polk, who made the announcement in his State of the Union message to Congress in December of 1848. The now-famous "Forty-Niner" gold rush was about to begin. Over the next seven years the non-Indian population of California escalated from 15,000 to over 300,000. And the economy went wild as the miners scraped more than $450 million in gold out of the hills and streams of northern California.

San Francisco mushroomed from a village to a major city, and with that growth came all the problems of trying to cope with too many people, too much money and too little law and order. In 1848, San Francisco had a population of just over 800 living in 200 houses. One year later, it had been transformed into a city of tents and shacks as thousands of gold-hungry men passed through en route to the gold fields, and others returned with the rewards of their labors. In addition to its reputation for being a no-holds-barred pleasure city, it also became a hotbed of racial discrimination and violence involving the Americans, Mexicans, Chinese and every other racial and ethnic group in residence. These conditions gave rise to vigilantism, which for a time seemed to be the predominant system of justice in the city... and the entire gold rush area.

Another city on which the gold strike had a dramatic effect was Sacramento. This was the site of Sutter's New Helvetia, but its name was changed in 1848 when it was formally laid out as a town. It then became the hub of all mining activities in the area. When California was admitted to the Union as the 31st state, and a free state under the Compromise of 1850, the first state legislature incorporated Sacramento as a city. It was made the state capital four years later.

California underwent another migration after the Civil War, when settlers were lured westward by the prospects of high wages and cheap land. By the end of the decade, the first transcontinental railroad, later to become part of the Southern Pacific, forged a link between Sacramento and the East, making California as accessible as any other state in the nation.

Blessed with an incredible endowment of natural resources, California has blossomed into a virtually self-sufficient cornucopia. Due to the wide range of soil, climate and water conditions throughout its borders, California leads the country in agriculture, growing more than 200 different crops. They include vegetables of every description, 70 kinds of fruits, several varieties of nuts, and staples like cotton and alfalfa.

California also ranks first in commercial fishing, with the harbor of Los Angeles at San Pedro being the nation's chief fishing port.

Though gold is today one of its lesser mineral assets, California is one of the nation's leading mining states. It produces a greater variety of minerals than any other state, and, in some cases, is the only source for a particular mineral in the United States. Such is the situation with boron. Most of the nation's supply of mercury as well as iodine comes from California. It ranks third in oil production and also has sizeable natural gas deposits.

High on the list of notable agricultural and economic achievements in California is the development and growth of the wine industry, located primarily in the Sonoma and Napa Valleys. Started a little more than 100 years ago, this industry now produces four out of every five bottles of wine sold in America, and its products are judged among the finest in the world. At the same time, Californians lead the country in their consumption of bourbon.

All is not perfect in paradise, however, and whatever largesse nature has bestowed on this favored land, nature can take back in a matter of seconds. For, below its surface, California is interlaced with a network of faults; cracks in the earth's crust, which, under pressure, can cause anything from a barely noticeable tremor to a full-fledged earthquake.

The principal fault of this network is the San Andreas Fault, a strike-slip fracture that runs at least 20 miles deep and extends about 650 miles from where it comes ashore near Point Arena in northwest California to the Gulf of California in the south. The San Andreas Fault is located on the boundary between two sections of the earth's crust – the Pacific plate and the North American plate – and actually separates southwest California from the North American continent. The Pacific plate moves northwest in relation to the rest of California, and geological evidence shows that this movement has covered approximately 350 miles over the past 30-60,000,000 years. Any movement along the fault will cause an earthquake, and thousands of harmless, minor quakes are recorded each year. Fortunately, very few quakes reach moderate intensity; even rarer is one of great intensity.

One of those rare occasions began on Wednesday, April 18, 1906. At 5.13 that morning, the first shock waves of a massive earthquake rumbled into a still sleeping city. Then, after a short pause of a few seconds, the quake shook the city again. In less than a minute and a half, the city of San Francisco was virtually destroyed. More than 600 people died in the quake and 250,000 were made homeless. Almost 500 blocks in the city were gutted by the quake and the ensuing fires, and the estimated loss of property ran to over $400 million.

San Francisco was not the only community to suffer the deadly effects of the quake. It was felt by every community along the San Andreas Fault for 400 miles. In some places, the land on the west side of the fault moved north by as much as 21 feet, while the land on the east did not move at all.

There have been two quakes of lesser severity since then, but they too have taken a toll in lives and property. Santa Barbara was struck in 1925 and sustained heavy property damage, and in 1933 Long Beach not only had property losses but there were 120 fatalities.

According to the best informed experts, there is a strong possibility that another serious earthquake is in the building stage. No one can predict exactly when, or where, this will occur, and most Californians can't bring themselves to believe there will be any more trouble in paradise. They prefer to dwell on the scenic wonders of their state rather than nature's aberration. And well they might.

Every state has its share of physical attributes and scenic beauty of which it can justifiably be proud. But California is different... California has *more* than its share, and most of it can only be described with superlatives.

Starting in the northernmost part of the state, at the Oregon border, and following the coast for about 450 miles as far south as Big Sur, live the world's most spectacular trees; the California or coast redwoods. The descendants of trees that inhabited large portions of the earth more than 30,000,000 years ago, some of those we see today are judged by experts to be more than 3,000 years old. Many of them grow to a height of 300 feet, the equivalent of a 30-story building, with the record at 367 feet and still standing. Their branches usually start about 100 feet above the ground and their trunks will measure from 10-20 feet in diameter.

The redwoods have made their last stand, so to speak, along the coast of northern and central California because the moist, warm climate and environment are extraordinarily suited to their needs. The heavy winter rains and the ocean fog that billows in from the Pacific all summer keep the trees cool, preventing dehydration. In addition, the soil is rich enough to give them sufficient sustenance.

The redwood has no enemies in nature, except, perhaps, man. Its fibrous, spongy bark, which may be 12 inches thick, makes the tree fire resistant. Its red wood is soft and weak but amazingly resistant to decay, disease or insects. Because of its durability, the wood is highly prized in the lumbering industry. One tree can be cut into 480,000 board feet of lumber worth thousands of dollars. Fortunately, conservationists were able to muster some protection for the redwoods before all of them fell to the ax and the saw. Today, of the nearly 2,000,000 acres once covered by redwoods, only about 300,000 acres of virgin trees are safely preserved within the confines of an extensive system of national and state parks.

Every year, swarms of tourists head north out of San Francisco towards Eureka and Crescent City on U.S. 101, the Redwood Highway, to enjoy the majestic splendor of nature's venerable giants.

To the uninitiated, there is some confusion about the difference between the California redwood and the giant sequoia, sometimes called the Sierra redwood.

The California redwood, *Sequoia sempervirens*, grows in the mountains on the Pacific coast. The giant sequoia, *Sequoiadendron giganteum*, grows only on the western slopes of the Sierra Nevada Mountains of California at altitudes of 5-7,000 feet. It doesn't grow as tall as its coastal cousin, but its trunk is usually much larger. Several sequoias have measured 100 feet around the base, with a diameter of approximately 37 feet. The world's largest tree in volume of wood is named the General Sherman, lives in Sequoia National park and is believed to be 3,500 years old. It stands 272.4 feet high, with a circumference of 101.6 feet. If this tree was harvested, it would weigh about 6,000 tons and yield the astonishing total of 600,000 board feet of timber.

Like the coast redwood, the sequoia is very durable and seems free from the natural ravages of age, disease and insect attack. Some of the largest trees have lost their tops to lightning, however.

As for the derivation of the name *sequoia*, it comes from a Cherokee Indian, *Sequoya*, who invented a written alphabet for his tribe.

Approaching San Francisco from the north, one of the most stirring and famous sights along the entire coast of California is the Golden Gate Bridge, which connects northern California to the peninsula of San Francisco. This magnificent structure is one of the world's largest suspension bridges, spanning the Golden Gate, a mile-wide channel that links the Pacific to San Francisco Bay, the largest natural harbor in the world. Nearby is the equally impressive, but lesser known, 8¼-mile Oaklands Bay Bridge; the longest bridge in the world over navigable water.

Built on and around 42 hills, this leading seaport of the Pacific Coast is renowned for its special charm, exciting terrain, unusual public transportation, fine restaurants, sophisticated cultural activities, and its moderate climate. Mark Twain once said in jest that the coldest winter he ever spent was a summer in San Francisco, but the relatively cool weather of a San Francisco summer has been an attraction rather than a deterrent to visitors.

San Francisco is noted for its waterfront, and much of the city's life revolves around it. There is an abundance of places for sightseeing, shopping and dining at such places as Fisherman's Wharf, Pier 39, the Cannery and Ghirardelli Square. Not to be overlooked is Golden

Gate Park, more than 1,000 acres of woods and lakes plus four museums and two athletic stadiums.

San Francisco is the insurance and financial capital of the West, with the world's largest bank (the Bank of America) headquartered there, and a stock exchange. And the city ranks with New York as a world communications center. The population is a broad mix of ethnic and racial groups, including the largest Chinese settlements outside the Orient.

The most breath-taking sights in California are not in the cities or suburbs but along the shoreline. And the best way to enjoy those sights is to take Highway 1, which follows the coast almost all the way down to Los Angeles. Be forewarned, however, that Highway 1 is not a multi-laned freeway but a narrow, winding, often preciptous ribbon of a road that will test the skill and mettle of the most adventurous driver. For example, just south of the community of Pacifica, below San Francisco, is a notorious three-mile stretch of road, 400 feet up, called Devil's Slide, where the cliff occasionally slips.

Further down the coast, at Pigeon Point, is the second tallest lighthouse in the country at 115 feet high. The point was named for the clipper ship, *Carrier Pigeon*, that went down there in 1853. After several more ships suffered the same fate, the lighthouse was erected in 1872.

A little south of Pigeon Point is Año Nuevo Point, where a rather startling spectacle takes place annually between mid-December and March. This area is an elephant-seal rookery, where those huge, lumbering, long-nosed animals come ashore to give birth and to mate. Once almost hunted to extinction by whalers who wanted their blubber, the elephant seals are now protected and their population has increased dramatically.

The elephant-seal season starts about mid-December, when the massive bulls – they range from 16 to 20 feet in length and weigh from three to four tons – come ashore and fight to establish territorial and mating rights. Lesser males are driven away, and the dominant bulls, known as beach masters, assemble their harems as the cows arrive in January to give birth to pups from last year's mating. This area has become such a popular attraction during the season that park rangers restrict open access and only allow guided walks to be conducted by naturalists in small groups. Reservations for these walks are recommended.

Further south is Santa Cruz, a seashore town that has some of the best weather in the area, plus a famous roller coaster ride and the last boardwalk on the California coast. Once a deteriorating retirement community, Santa Cruz was revitalized by the establishment of a University of California campus, which not only brought in an influx of young people to balance the population but also a surge of small arts-and-crafts businesses. The new demand for housing has resulted in the salvaging and refurbishing of many of the wonderful old Victorian houses that give the community a special ambiance. One more item of note: more than 95% of the nation's Brussels sprouts are produced in this area.

Following Highway 1 around Monterey Bay, en route to the Monterey Peninsula, the countryside becomes some of the finest farmland in the United States. Here, in the Salinas Valley, proclaimed the "Salad Bowl of the Nation," and the Monterey Bay Shore, are grown crops worth more than $500 million annually. They include lettuce, artichokes, sugar beets and grapes. The Salinas River, which waters the valley and flows into the bay, is known locally as the "upside-down-river" because it flows south to north, is fed principally from underground sources, and disappears for the most part underground during the summer.

Literary aficionados, and especially fans of John Steinbeck, will recognize this part of California as Steinbeck country, the setting for so many of his novels. Steinbeck was born in Salinas and is buried there. His birthplace, a fine 1897 Victorian frame house, has been preserved and is open for luncheon. The public library, which was renamed for Steinbeck in 1969, holds an annual festival in August and has some of his manuscripts and memorabilia on display.

The Monterey Peninsula. Many have come here with a "show me" attitude – it attracts three to four million visitors a year – and few have failed to be beguiled by its natural beauty, the haunting serenity of its vistas, the elegance and charm that permeates the life styles of its communities.

Once the Spanish capital of Alta California, Monterey always seemed to be something special from the time it was discovered in 1602 by Sebastian Viscaino, who could not contain his enthusiasm for the mildness of the climate, the fertility of the soil, the abundance of game. He called it "the best port that could be desired."

More than 200 years later, after Richard Henry Dana visited there as a crewman aboard the brig *Pilgrim* out of Boston, he wrote in his odyssey, *Two Years before The Mast*, "Monterey is decidedly the pleasantest and most civilized-looking place in California."

Robert Louis Stevenson lived at Monterey for four months late in 1879 and became fascinated with the ocean and the shoreline. In his essay, *Monterey*, he wrote, "the one common note of all this country is the haunting presence of the ocean..."

And he also wrote, "a great faint sound of breakers follows you high up into the inland canyons; the roar of water dwells in the clean, empty rooms of Monterey as in a shell upon the chimney; go where you will, you have but to pause and listen to hear the voice of the Pacific."

One of three communities on the Peninsula, the town of Monterey is a happy mix of past and present. Much of its Mexican and Spanish heritage has been preserved architecturally along with the later Yankee influence of the New England settlers who came here around the Horn. And Cannery Row, that once malodorous and depressing collection of sardine factories that was the setting for two of John Steinbeck's more graphic novels, *Cannery Row* and *Sweet Thursday*, has been transformed into a tourist attraction of shops, art galleries and restaurants.

Pacific Grove, on the northern tip of the peninsula, had its beginning as a religious retreat. It was founded in 1875 by a group of Methodist Episcopal ministers from San Francisco as a summer resort for Christian people. At first, the resort consisted of rows of tents, pitched beneath the pines, which could be rented by the week. Strict abstinence from drinking, dancing and any other form of sin or vice was enforced, with lights out at 9 p.m. Gradually, more permanent residences began to appear, and in 1889 the city of Pacific Grove was incorporated. The blue laws remained in effect until they were voted out in 1969.

Today, Pacific Grove is known for a different type of congregation. It is now known as the "Butterfly Town U.S.A." Every winter millions of monarch butterflies migrate to the area, settling in selected groves of pine, oak, cypress and eucalyptus from November to March. To honor this happening, the city erected a statue to the butterfly and holds an annual parade in October which features thousands of children outfitted with orange and black wings. And there is a city ordinance imposing a $500 fine for molesting or interfering with the monarchs. On sunny days, butterfly watchers are treated to the unusual sight of waves of brilliant color drifting over gardens and groves as the butterflies take wing in search of food. On overcast, cool days, they are somnolent.

The third of the Monterey triumvirate, located at the south end of the peninsula, is Carmel... full name, Carmel-by-the-Sea. It was once a colony for writers and artists, and the community still tries to preserve some of that Bohemian chic. One of its long-time residents was the poet Robinson Jeffers, who lived in self-imposed isolation at Tor House and Hawk Tower, which he built of stone with his own hands. Other talented people who were either short-term settlers or visitors included Jack London, Sinclair Lewis, Upton Sinclair, Lincoln Steffens, Mary Austin, and photographers Edward Weston and Ansel Adams.

Today, Carmel is a very posh little community of approximately 5,000 whose wealth and desire for privacy have kept land prices up and development down. Though Carmel residents often complain about the crowds of tourists, the town boasts a profusion of expensive boutiques, galleries and smart little restaurants that would not survive without the business brought in by outsiders. Nevertheless, commercial signs are kept small and inconspicuous. There are no traffic lights in the commercial section, no parking meters or garages either. There is no courthouse, jail, mortuary or cemetery... not even a school within the village limits. There is no mail delivery because the houses have no numbers, so everyone goes to the post office to collect mail... and to socialize.

Aside from its little eccentricities, Carmel does have one of the world's most perfect beaches, a stretch of unmatched white sand ringed by Monterey pines and weather-warped cypresses that make it exceptional even for the California coast. And as a reminder of its Spanish origin, there is the Mission San Carlos Borromeo de Carmelo, whose first structure was built by Father Serra in 1771. The mission was designated a basilica by Pope John XXIII, one of only two in the western United States.

No visit to the Monterey Peninsula would be complete without a ride on 17-Mile Drive through the Del Monte Forest and the fabled area known as Pebble Beach. Located between Monterey to the north, Carmel to the south and the Pacific to the west, the forest and environs has been a playground for the rich and powerful ever since railroad magnate Charles Crocker opened the Hotel Del Monte in 1880. Labeled "Crocker's Folly" by its detractors, the rambling but palatial hotel nevertheless became a gathering place for millionaires and political moguls, including two U.S. presidents, Benjamin Harrison and Teddy Roosevelt.

The area did not begin to fulfill its potential until Samuel F. B. Morse, grandnephew of the inventor and painter, took over the 20,000-acre parcel. He changed the 17-Mile Drive to its current route, planned golf courses, trails, bridle paths, roads, conservation areas and built the accommodation, now called the Lodge, at Pebble Beach to replace the old hotel. He then invited selected people of wealth to build homes within the property. Today, Pebble Beach in the Del Monte Forest is a private enclave of 5,300 acres with less than 6,000 residents. The only access to the area is through one of four toll gates. The public is admitted for a $4.00 toll, which is refundable upon checking into the Lodge.

Of the three major golf courses, the best known is Pebble Beach because of its annual television exposure as the site of the Bing Crosby tournament. Probably no golf hole has been photographed more often than the 18th at Pebble Beach which runs atop a bluff paralleling the Pacific.

The course called Spyglass Hill might appeal more to literary golfers because it was named by Samuel Morse in tribute to Robert Louis Stevenson's *Treasure Island*. Stevenson completed the book three years after his stay at Monterey, and it is believed that his fictional settings were influenced by that visit. So, each of the holes at Spyglass is named after someone or something in the book.

The third course, Cypress Point, is also extremely scenic, and although the first two courses are open to the public, Cypress Point is one of the world's most exclusive clubs.

For most people, the ride along 17-Mile Drive provides a rare view of the ambiance and life style that only the very wealthy can afford. As some irreverent observer once said, "it's what God would have done if He'd had money."

Leaving Carmel behind and heading south, Highway 1 crosses the Carmel River and soon passes the last residences of the wealthy at Carmel Highlands. From then until the narrow, two-lane road reaches San Simeon, 90-plus miles away, it is Big Sur country, that spectacular meeting of the Santa Lucia Mountains and the Pacific described by Robinson Jeffers as that "jagged country which nothing but a falling meteor will ever plow." But before venturing into Big Sur, there is one stop that the traveler should make – Point Lobos State Reserve.

Contained within this small promontory are just under 1,300 acres of unadulterated beauty comprised of more than 300 plant species ranging from delicate buttercups to the symbolic Monterey cypress. This is the home of more than 250 species of birds and animals, including two species of sea lions for whom the Spaniards named the peninsula (Punta de los Lobos Marinos... Point of the Sea Wolves). Also seen in the waters off the point are harbor seals, killer whales, sea otters and two species of cormorant. In recent years, about 750 acres of submerged land were added to the area, making it the first underwater ecological reserve in the country.

Big Sur, an area that 20-year resident author Henry Miller described as "a region where one is always conscious of the weather, of space, of grandeur and eloquent silence," is a place one goes to for its rugged, unspoiled isolation... not casual amusement or diversion. For decades after its discovery by the Spanish, this area was virtually uninhabited, being accessible only by a treacherous horse trail. It took its name from the first ranch that was established in 1834 – Juan Bautista Alvarado's *El Sur*, which translates to "south of Monterey." Construction on the first paved road did not start until 1920, and only then with the help of convict labor. It did not reach San Simeon until 17 years later. There was no electricity in the area until the 1950s.

Even today, there are fewer than 2,000 permanent residents on Big Sur, partly because of the lack of water and sewage facilities, but also because the watchdog Coastal Commission keeps a close rein on development plans. However, the tourist traffic on Highway 1 between Carmel and San Simeon has been increasing constantly and is estimated at two million cars a year.

In addition to the hardy handful who put such a high price on their privacy, there are several contemplative institutions that have sought out the solitude of Big Sur. They are the Esalen Institute, a leader in the "human potential" movement, a Carmelite monastery, a Benedictine hermitage, and the Tassajara Zen Center.

The latter, started in 1966 at Tassajara Hot Springs by the San Francisco Zen Center, is the largest Zen training center outside Japan. It is semi-monastic, and takes married and single students who stay for an average of three years. A unique feature of the center is that from May 1 through the summer it also becomes a hot-springs resort. It can accommodate 55-65 guests who want peace and quiet, good vegetarian cooking, lots of walking and hiking and access to the hot springs. The resort has no phones, electricity, entertainment of any kind, or bar. Overnighters and day visitors are welcome by reservation only.

Anyone looking for the village of Big Sur to match the chic of Carmel will be greatly disappointed. After passing a roadsign announcing Big Sur, the road will go past clusters of roadside structures huddled under the redwoods for the next six miles... that's downtown Bug Sur Village in Big Sur Valley.

Other points of interest to watch for on Highway 1 are: the Bixby Creek bridge, a 700-foot concrete-arch span that is 265 feet above the creek; the Point Sur Light Station, whose million candlepower light flashes every 15 seconds and can be seen 25 miles at sea; the nine-acre town of Gorda (population 20), named for an offshore rock the Spanish thought looked like a voluptuous lady.

By continuing down Highway 1, the next point of interest reached is San Simeon, site of *La Cuesta Encantada*, The Enchanted Hill, the utterly incredible castle that William Randolph Hearst built in the Santa Lucia foothills. The estate, now officially known as the Hearst San Simeon State Historical Monument, once extended for 50 miles along the coast and 10 miles inland, a total of 265,000 acres.

Much of the land was acquired by George Hearst, William's father and a senator from the state of California, at 60 and 70 cents an acre as early as 1865. The elder Hearst set up a working ranch there, stocked with prize cattle, and also used it for recreational hunting, fishing, riding and camping. George Hearst had made his fortune in mining, but William, his only child, achieved even greater wealth and power as the owner of the world's biggest media empire. And it all began in 1887, when George Hearst gave his son a newspaper, the *San Francisco Examiner*. At the height of his power, William owned 29 newspapers, 15 magazines, 8 radio stations and 4 film companies.

In 1919, his mother bequeathed him the ranch, and William began building his dream castle, a project that would not be completed even after 20 years and the expenditure of untold millions of dollars. As the principal architect Hearst hired Julia Morgan, the first woman civil engineering graduate at Berkeley (1894) and the first female graduate of the Ecole des Beaux-Arts in Paris (1902). The project was still going on when Julia Morgan retired and turned the job over to her assistant.

The castle, basically Spanish-Moorish with twin towers, is poured reinforced concrete with a facing of Utah limestone. It contains more than 100 rooms, and it was never completed because Hearst was never totally satisfied, always demanding changes or additions. It is estimated that Hearst spent upwards of $30 million just furnishing the castle. He had agents roaming the world, purchasing the entire contents of estates and other castles. On two occasions Hearst bought a complete Spanish cloister and a Cistercian monastery. And he was known to outbid the world's wealthiest collectors for antiques and objets d'art that he desired.

The outside grounds were just as elaborate, with formal gardens, pools (one of them, the 104-foot Neptune Pool, is surrounded by Etruscan-style colonnades and backed by a Greco-Roman temple), a zoo and a game preserve. The gardens alone required the services of 20 gardeners, who generally worked at night because Hearst did not like to see workmen on the grounds. It has also been said that the gardeners once painted the yellowing fronds of a dying palm tree green until Hearst was away and they could replace it. One of Hearst's phobias was of death in any form and under any circumstances.

Hearst had a great fondness for animals, which he gratified by having the world's largest private menagerie as well as a game preserve with about 90 species of free-roaming animals. He also maintained farms for cattle, dairy and poultry, and bred blooded horses.

Moving into the partially completed castle in 1924, Hearst, along with his hostess, actress Marion Davies, usually entertained upwards of 50 guests a weekend. Some were flown in the Hearst plane to the castle's private landing strip which was equipped with the world's first private-field instrument landing system. Other guests would be taken by Hearst's private train to San Luis Obispo, where a fleet of limousines would wait to drive them to San Simeon.

Despite his unstinting extravagances about everything else, one of Hearst's eccentricities was his insistence on having his dining table set with paper napkins instead of linen. And the condiments were served in their original containers... just like at a picnic.

No one in the world, not even William Randolph Hearst, could continue to spend money at the rate he did, and by 1937 he was on the verge of bankruptcy. He was forced to sell off pieces of his media empire and many of his antique and art collections. The U.S. government bought 164,000 acres of ranchland for troop training at the onset of World War II.

Hearst closed the castle during the war for fear it would be shelled by enemy submarines and reopened it briefly after the war. He had a heart attack in 1947 and died four years later.

After Hearst's death, no one could afford to maintain the castle, so in 1957 the State Department of Parks and Recreation took it over along with 123 acres. It has been open to the public ever since, and nearly a million people a year take one of the four two-hour guided tours (reservations only). The Hearst castle is one stop that should be on every visitor's itinerary.

Not long after leaving San Simeon, the shoreline becomes less rugged, untamed and exciting. From Point Conception, where the land swings eastward before turning south again, down to the Mexican border, lies Southern California, a favored part of the globe that has become synonymous with the "good life" – a land of golden sunshine, balmy climate, endless beaches within easy reach of snow-capped mountains, beautiful people and fertile soil.

The major city in this area is Los Angeles, once an adobe pueblo dating back to 1781 and now a sprawling metropolis of more than 450 square miles, about ten times the size of San Francisco. Its harbor on San Pedro Bay is the largest man-made harbor in the world, with 28 miles of sheltered area for freighters and passenger ships. It is also home to more than 400 commercial fishing boats.

In addition to being the market and shipping center for Los Angeles County, one of the richest farm counties in the country, Los Angeles is second only to Detroit in the production of cars and second only to Akron, Ohio, in the production of rubber and tires. It ranks second to Chicago in furniture making and second to New York in creating women's dresses, but first in the production of sports clothes. It stands third in oil refining.

The industry that really made Los Angeles famous, however, is the motion picture business. The first commercial film to be made in California, *The Count of Monte Cristo*, was completed in Los Angeles in 1907. Three years later, Hollywood had become the motion picture capital of the world. At one time, nine-tenths of all American films were made in Hollywood, and though its glitter has been somewhat dulled by the decline of the great studios and the star system, it still retains its title as the film capital. Every year, thousands of visitors are attracted to this land of make-believe and tour the operating studios. Recently, a major portion of the television industry has also made its home in the area.

Other points of interest in Los Angeles are Hancock Park, which contains the La Brea Tar Pits, and the 4,000-acre Griffith Park, one of the largest city parks in the country, which houses the Los Angeles Zoo. About 25 miles southeast of downtown Los Angeles, at Anaheim, is the world-famous Disneyland.

Lying offshore are eight Channel Islands that help form the Santa Barbara and San Pedro Channels. One of them, Catalina Island, about 24 miles off shore, was discovered by Juan Rodriguez Cabrillo in 1542 and named Santa Catalina in honor of Saint Catherine. One-time home of Spanish pirates, much of the island was bought in the 1920s by the late William Wrigley, Jr., and developed as a tourist resort, which it has remained ever since. The beautiful island is a favorite among sport fishermen.

Perhaps the most famous single event to take place annually in the Los Angeles area is the Parade of Roses on New Year's Day at nearby Pasadena. The parade is part of Pasadena's Tournament of Roses and was modeled after the Carnival of Flowers at Nice, France. The tournament is climaxed by the playing of the Rose Bowl football game.

South of Los Angeles, on the coast at Palos Verdes Estates, is the world's largest oceanarium, the Marineland of the Pacific, with 5,000 marine specimens.

About 60 miles southeast of Los Angeles is San Juan Capistrano, founded as a mission in 1776, when the American colonies were fighting for their freedom from English rule. Today, the mission is known world-wide as the place where the swallows return on March 19 after wintering in the south. And close by is San Clemente, once the home of former President Richard M. Nixon.

Further down the coast lies San Diego, sometimes called *The Cradle of California Civilization*. First discovered by Cabrillo when he sailed into the bay in 1542, it was not touched by Western civilization until 1769, when Father Serra established his first mission, San Diego de Alcala, there. Because of its natural deepwater port, one of the best in the country, and balmy climate, San Diego flourished and soon became the center of the Pacific hide trade. It was organized as a town in 1834, and incorporated as a city in 1850, the year that California became a state.

Today, San Diego is one of the most important naval centers in the United States, employing thousands of government workers. The navy's largest air station on the Pacific Coast is housed on North Island in the bay.

The major industries in the area, other than government business, are agriculture (San Diego County leads the world in the production of avocados), commercial fishing and canning (primarily tuna),

shipbuilding, airplane and missile production and electronics.

San Diego's Balboa Park, in the heart of the city, contains the renowned San Diego Zoological Gardens, one of the world's largest zoos. It has 4,000 animals plus 100 acres of semitropical trees and flowers. Surrounding the city are the fashionable resort areas of Coronado, La Jolla, Mission Bay Aquatic Park and Oceanside, making the region very popular with vacationers... and retired people.

Just 16 miles further south, the journey down the California coast ends at the border with Mexico. Few, if any other states, can offer the traveler the range of sights, sounds, climates, points of interest and variety of life styles that this most-populous of states does. And what we have seen is just a good beginning. California has four national parks (Kings Canyon, Lassen Volcanic, Sequoia and Yosemite), 22 national forests, 13 national wilderness areas. It also has eight national monuments: Cabrillo, Channel Islands, Death Valley (partly in Nevada), Devils Postpile, Joshua Tree, Lava Beds, Muir Woods and Pinnacles. Winding through the parks are thousands of miles of trails, including the 175-mile-long John Muir Trail along the Sierra Nevadas.

Yosemite has several of the highest waterfalls in North America, with Ribbon Falls, (1,612 feet) being the highest on the continent. Of California's 8,000 lakes, Lake Tahoe is the deepest, averaging 1,500 feet in depth.

With so much of its natural grandeur still unspoiled, it's little wonder that California is an irresistible lure for vacationers looking for something new, different and exciting. And once enthralled by the California mystique, some never go home again.

Previous page: the curiously shaped cliffs of Cabrillo National Monument on Point Loma, San Diego. Above: an evening view across San Diego Bay towards the gleaming buildings of the downtown district. Facing page: yachts at anchor in Monterey Harbor. Overleaf: (left) Seaport Village and (right) Coronado Hotel, both in San Diego.

Some miles north of San Diego, but still within the city limits, is the town of La Jolla (these pages and overleaf, right). The small, sandy beaches and coves which abound here have made La Jolla a mecca for all those interested in sunbathing and water sports. Overleaf left: Coronado Marina, backed by the graceful sweep of the San Diego-Coronado Bay Bridge.

When Juan Rodriguez Cabrillo sighted the shores that would become San Diego in 1542, the great Pacific rollers had been smashing against the shore for millions of years. Where the pounding waves meet the land they have carved many strange rock formations as at Windansea Beach (above and overleaf, right), Bird Rock (facing page) and Sunset Cliffs (overleaf, left).

Above: Santa Monica, whose fabulous beach lies within the widespread bounds of Los Angeles. Facing page: the palm-fringed sands of Venice, another coastal town now swallowed up by Los Angeles. Overleaf: the 4th of July celebrations give Californians an excuse to take to the sea in a wide variety of craft.

Above and overleaf, left: the long beach of Malibu, which reaches from Los Angeles to the extreme edge of Ventura County. Facing page and overleaf, right: two views of evening at the town of Santa Monica, whose waving palms and broad, sandy beach draw visitors from across the state and the nation.

Above: some of the many beach houses which line the shore at Malibu. Facing page: at the Pacific Palisades an engineered stream reaches the beach, where natural forces have banked up the sand and forced it to change its course dramatically before entering the sea. Overleaf: (left) a view of large, anchored ships from Los Angeles Port Scenic Drive and (right) Santa Monica.

These pages and overleaf, right: Santa Monica, which has long been a resort for the citizens of Los Angeles.
The potential of its three-mile-long beach and magnificent, year-round climate was realized as long ago as
1870. Overleaf, left: Newport Beach, 40 miles to the southeast.

Above: the Pacific Palisades. Facing page: the British liner Queen Mary, which was launched in 1934 and led an eventful life, including a period as a troopship, before being retired to Long Beach in 1967. She is now open to the public and houses several museums and exhibits as well as an hotel. Overleaf: (left) Santa Barbara and (right) a view from the slopes above nearby Avila Beach.

46

Pfeiffer Beach (these pages and overleaf) is located just south of the entrance to the Pfeiffer-Big Sur State Park. It is approached through the narrow Sycamore Canyon Road from State Highway 1, itself a very picturesque route.

Above: the Cabrillo Highway, named after the man who discovered the region, runs along the coast south of Carmel, below folded hills which dwarf the works of man. At Bixby Creek (facing page and overleaf, left) Highway 1 arcs over a graceful bridge some 260 feet above the water. Overleaf, right: a view south towards Point Sur.

Driving south from Carmel, State 1 clings to the edges of cliffs, pitching and dipping and providing the motorist with astonishingly lovely sea views. Bixby Creek Bridge, pictured from several angles (these pages and overleaf, left), carries the road high above the creek. Overleaf, right: nearby scenery.

Perhaps nowhere else in Calfornia is the coastline so varied and so beautiful within such a small area as along the strip of land around Big Sur (these pages and overleaf), the landscape varying from the sandy beach at Sand Dollar (above) and the low rocks at Piedras Blancas (overleaf, right) to the jagged headlands (facing page) and those above Limekiln Beach (overleaf, left).

Big Sur and Monterey Peninsula's coastlines are studded with crags and rocks (these pages and overleaf) which have proven to be the ruin of many a ship on its way to safe harbor in Monterey Bay.

Above: black and heavy storm clouds blot out the sun's rays at Point Sur. Facing page: the sun bejewels the sea at China Cove, Point Lobos State Reserve. The cove is part of a protected promontory of 1,250 acres and enfolds the only beach in the reserve safe for swimmers. Overleaf: precariously perched clifftop buildings along the Big Sur coastline.

The small town of Carmel, south of Cypress Point, has a reputation for unusual shops, but is probably best known for the Carmel River State Beach (these pages and overleaf) which attracts people from far and wide with its fine sands and romantic, rocky scenery.

On the foreshore of Carmel Beach gnarled and rare Monterey Cypress trees frame two strollers on the sand. Surf and undercurrents make this a hazardous beach from which to swim, although it is a pleasant place to while away the day. Overleaf: two views of the rugged Big Sur coastline, (left) at Mill Creek and (right) at Julia Pfeiffer-Burns Park.

Looping west from Pacific Grove is one of the most scenically impressive stretches of road in California. The famed 17-mile Drive runs around the Monterey Peninsula to take in such sights as Cypress Point (above) and the rock-strewn headland (facing page). The drive ends at Carmel, where Pacific rollers crash to shore in a welter of spray (overleaf).

South of the Monterey Peninsula, but not far enough south to be part of Big Sur proper, is Point Lobos. This state reserve of some 1,200 acres encompasses some dramatic cliffs and offshore rocks, (above) Sea Lion Cove, as well as a splendid grove of Monterey Cypresses (facing page).

The Lone Cypress (facing page) stands a solitary sentinel at Sunset Point, near Monterey. At Point Lobos (overleaf, right) skeletal trees rear upwards from the cliff's edge like multi-pointed stag antlers, with the sea churned to froth against sun dappled rocks (above and overleaf, left).

Facing page: Gray Whale Cove, north of Montara, with its unspoilt beach. Above: Point Lobos State Reserve, whose famous stands of Monterey Cypress are pictured overleaf. This cypress, known scientifically as *Cupressus macrocarpa*, has wood which is hard and resistant but its use is limited by its rather unpleasant odor.

Facing page: the golf course on Cypress Point. The Monterey Peninsula is not only one of the loveliest areas south of San Francisco, it is also one of the richest in wildlife; (above) birds and seals on Scal Rocks, (overleaf, left) a rare sea otter in its characteristic sleeping posture, floating on its back and wrapped in a strand of kelp, and (overleaf, right) a seal with its pup.

The Pebble Beach area of the Monterey Peninsula is one of outstanding beauty. Here there are the three famous golf courses, Spyglass Hill, Cypress Point (facing page) and Pebble Beach (above and overleaf), each set amid scenery unmatched elsewhere in the nation, with rolling ocean and shady forest close to hand.

The town of Monterey (these pages and overleaf), with its magnificent bay, was chosen by the Spaniards as the capital of Alta California, and remained so under the Mexican flag. The commercial fishing boats which kept the town busy half a century ago have now been replaced by the pleasure craft which crowd the bay and marina, while Fisherman's Wharf (above) has gained shops, an art gallery and a theater.

Above: Lovers' Point at Pacific Grove provides a wealth of color as a carpet of mauve blooms covers the shoreline and a tranquil, blue sea runs to the horizon; a sea which takes on a more turbulent and spume-splattered mood at Monterey Beach (facing page).

The most beautiful bay on all the California coast is that known as San Francisco Bay, and on the shores of the bay stands perhaps the most wonderful city in the nation. San Francisco (these pages) is linked to its suburbs by the Oakland Bay (these pages and overleaf, left) and Golden Gate (overleaf, right) Bridges, over which pour thousands of vehicles trying to get around the inconvenient shoreline.

San Francisco's Fisherman's Wharf (above) attracts thousands of visitors every year with its shops, restaurants and quaintness. Facing page and overleaf, left: the Golden Gate Bridge opened in 1937 amid much controversy as to whether it would mar the beauty of the bay, but it has since proved to be both beautiful and necessary. Overleaf right: moorings near the city.

In 1579 Sir Francis Drake landed on a coast he called New Albion and which he claimed for Elizabeth I of England. Just where he landed has long been disputed, but it is believed to have been in the region of Point Reyes National Seashore: (above) the Point Reyes Lighthouse and (facing page) a view from Chimney Rock. Overleaf: (left) Smugglers Cove, north of Gualala, and (right) Sonoma Coast.

Above: some of the craft in the harbor at Bodega Bay, an active fishing port west of Santa Rosa. Facing page: the picturesque, rocky shore of Salt Point, north of Fort Ross. Overleaf: (left) a rugged bay north of Elk and (right) the beautiful, open sands of Big River Beach at Mendocino.

Above: driftwood scattered along the sands at Elk Cove, north of Elk. Facing page: the thin trickle of water that is Elk Creek runs over the sands to reach the Pacific, south of Mendocino.

INDEX